Note to Parents and Teachers

The READING ABOUT: STARTERS series introduces key science vocabulary to young children while encouraging them to discover and understand the world around them. The series works as a set of graded readers in three levels.

LEVEL 2: BEGIN TO READ ALONE follows guidelines set out in the National Curriculum for Year 2 in schools. These books can be read alone or as part of guided or group reading. Each book has three sections:

• Information pages that introduce key words. These key words appear in bold for easy recognition on pages where the related science concepts are explained.
• A lively story that recalls this vocabulary and encourages children to use these words when they talk and write.
• A quiz and index ask children to look back and recall what they have read.

Questions for Further Investigation

FROG to TADPOLE explains key concepts about LIFE CYCLES. Here are some suggestions for further discussion linked to the questions on the information spreads:

p. 5 *What do you need to grow?* All young animals need food to help them grow, e.g. a mother feeds her baby milk. A baby also needs lots of sleep while it is growing fast.

p. 7 *What other young animal names do you know?* As well as mammals, e.g. lamb, piglet, kitten, suggest birds, e.g. chick and cygnet, and insects, e.g. grubs and larvae.

p. 9 *What other eggs have you seen?* Discuss colour, shape and size. Bird/tortoise eggs have a hard shell, snake eggs are soft and leathery. Could mention care of wild birds' eggs.

p. 11 *How does an adult human keep a baby safe?* Discuss care of baby, e.g. feeding, keeping it warm and clean, and protecting from danger, e.g. swallowing, need for cot/pram.

p. 13 *How long does a human baby take to grow as big as its mother?* Could mention comparisons: crocodile matures in 2-3 years, some insects mature in about 10 days.

p. 15 *What must a chick grow or learn before it is an adult?* It must grow feathers, learn to fly/swim/hunt. Could ask what other young animals need to grow/learn to be adults.

p. 19 *How many stages are there in a butterfly's life?* Four: egg, caterpillar, pupa, butterfly. Three stages for frog: frogspawn, tadpole, adult. Two stages for human: young and adult.

p. 21 *Can you think of any stages in the life of a plant?* e.g. seed, seedling, adult plant.

p. 23 *How do people change as they grow old?* e.g. changes to hair, mobility, senses. Could encourage children to talk to grandparents about their lives/growing older.

ADVISORY TEAM

Educational Consultant
Andrea Bright – Science Co-ordinator, Trafalgar Junior School, Twickenham

Literacy Consultant
Jackie Holderness – former Senior Lecturer in Primary Education, Westminster Institute, Oxford Brookes University

Series Consultants
Anne Fussell – Early Years Teacher and University Tutor, Westminster Institute, Oxford Brookes University

David Fussell – C.Chem., FRSC

CONTENTS

© Aladdin Books Ltd 2005

Designed and produced by
Aladdin Books Ltd
2/3 Fitzroy Mews
London W1T 6DF

First published in
Great Britain in 2005 by
Franklin Watts
96 Leonard Street
London EC2A 4XD

A catalogue record for this book is available from the British Library.

ISBN 0 7496 6248 4

Printed in Malaysia

All rights reserved

Editor: Sally Hewitt

Design: Flick, Book Design and Graphics

Thanks to:
• The pupils of Trafalgar Infants School, Twickenham for appearing as models in this book.
• Chloé and Clara Guerif and Hilary Harrison for appearing as models in the story.
• The pupils and teachers of Trafalgar Junior School, Twickenham and St. Nicholas C.E. Infant School, Wallingford, for testing the sample books.

Photocredits:
l-left, r-right, b-bottom, t-top, c-centre, m-middle
Cover tl, 12tr, 21 both — Ingram Publishing. Cover tc, 12b, 13b, 23b — Comstock. Cover tr, 13tl — Brand X Pictures. Cover b, 4br — Digital Vision. 2tl, 7tr, 7b, 22 both, 23tr, 24bl, 25bl, 29b — Corbis. 2ml, 4bl, 5b, 9b, 19tl, 32 — Corel. 2bl, 14-15 all, 28t (cut out), 31bm — Stockbyte. 3, 16 both, 17tr, 26mr, 27bl, 28b, 30t — David Jones. 5t both — PBD. 6tr, 10tl, 20b — Ken Hammond /USDA. 6b, 10b, 20tr, 31tr — Scott Bauer/ USDA. 8 both, 9t, 11tl, 17b, 19b, 31tr, 31ml — US Fish & Wildlife Service. 11b — Flick Smith. 18, 31br — USDA. 24tl, 24mr, 25mr, 26tl, 26bl, 27tr, 27mr, 29t, 31bl — Jim Pipe. 25tl — John Foxx Images. 28t (inset) — Otto Rogge.

READING ABOUT

Starters

GROWTH AND LIFE CYCLES

Tadpole to Frog

By Jim Pipe

Aladdin/Watts
London • Sydney

All living things **grow**. **Adult** animals have **young**. The **young grow** up into **adults**.

Some animals don't change much as they **grow**. A child looks like its **parents**. So does a **young** horse, a foal.

Horse and foal

4

Some animals change a lot as they **grow** up. They don't look like their **parents**.

Can you guess what this hairy **young** animal will **grow** into?

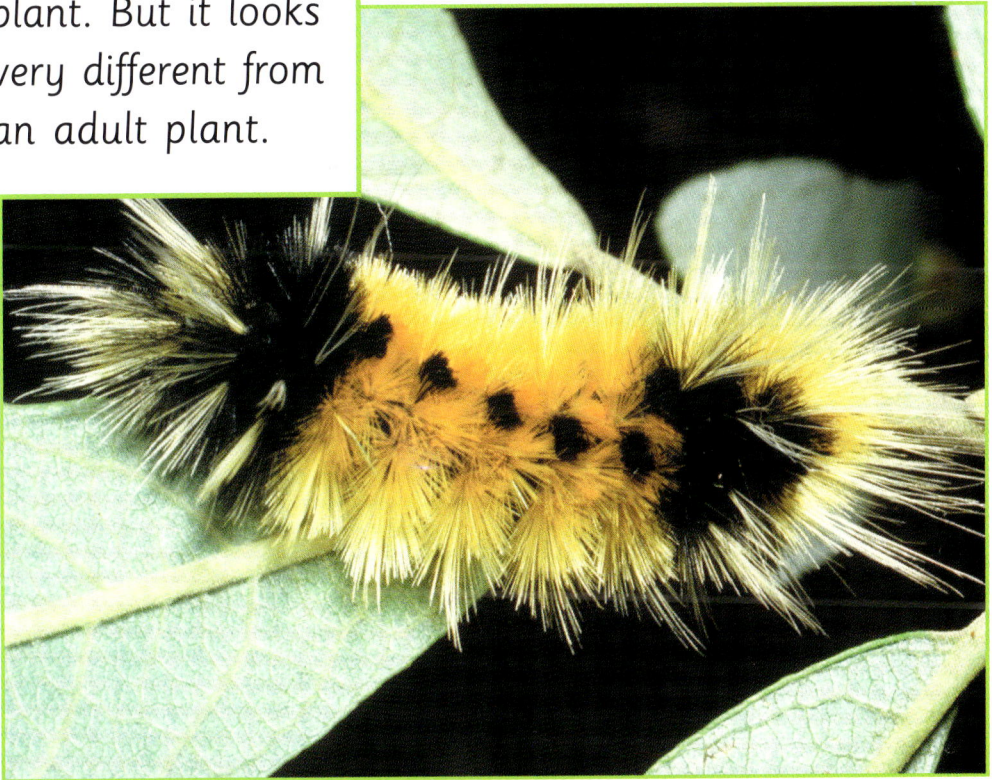

A seed grows into a plant. But it looks very different from an adult plant.

Like you, some animals start life inside their **mother**. They grow inside her body.

Then the **mother** gives **birth** and they are **born**.

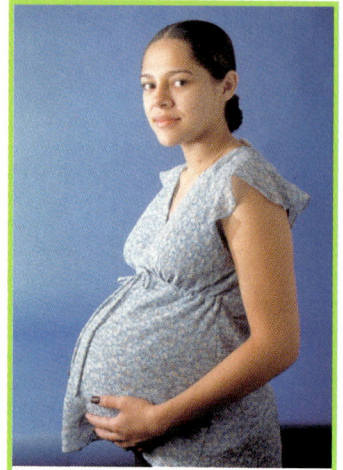

A mother with a baby inside her is pregnant.

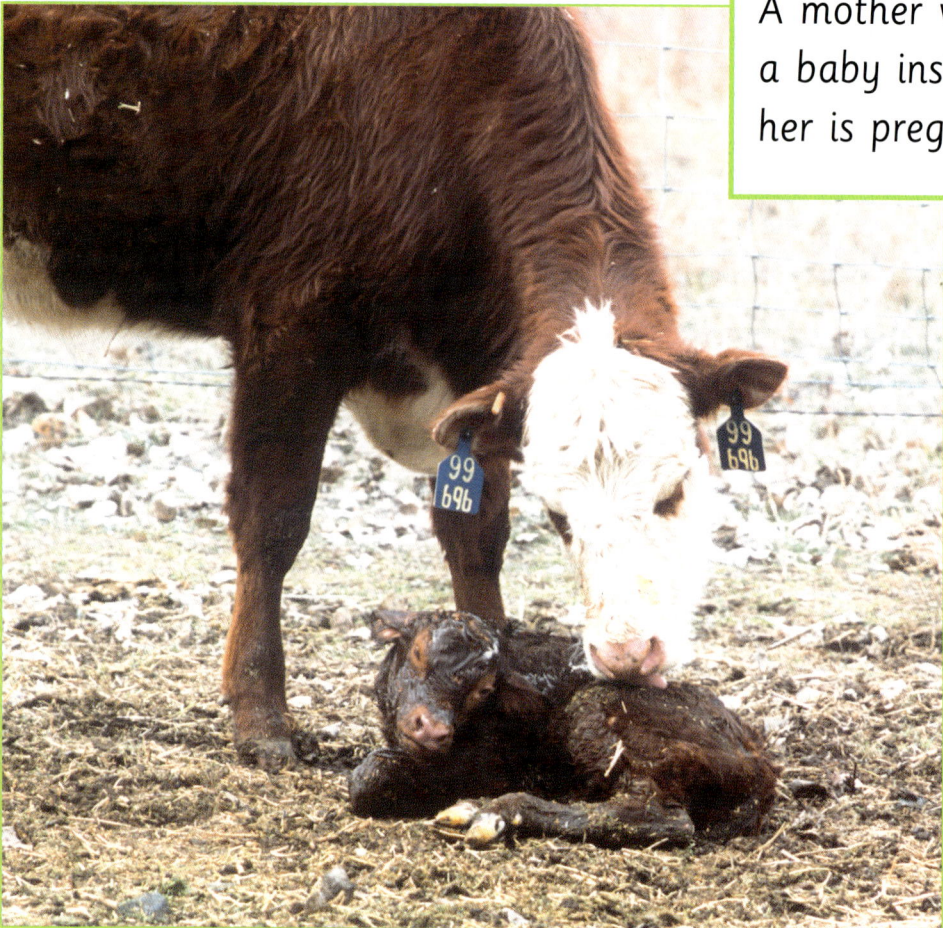

Cow and calf

6

Hairy animals like dogs, bears and sheep are **born**. They are animals called **mammals**. People are **mammals**, too.

Young **mammals**, have special names like calf, foal, fawn and cub.

Polar bear and cub

Deer and fawn

• What other young animal names do you know?

Most animals are not like mammals.
They start life inside an **egg**. The **egg**
gives them food to grow.

Birds, fish, snails and ants
all **lay eggs**. The **eggs** pop
out of a part of their body.

Duck's eggs

This snail is laying tiny white eggs.

8

Hatching

When they are big enough, the young break open the **egg**. They **hatch** out of the **egg**.

Snakes, crocodiles and turtles **hatch** from **eggs**, too.

• What other eggs have you seen?

A mother **cares** for her **baby**. She keeps it warm. She feeds her baby **milk**, the food it needs to grow.

Pig and piglet

Some animal mothers care for their young, too. A mother pig feeds her piglet **milk**.

10

Most young fish are not cared for by their parents.

Many animals do not **care** for their young. A turtle lays its eggs on a beach, then leaves them.

After it hatches, a young turtle lives on its own. It must find its own food.

Young turtles

• How does an adult human keep a baby safe?

A young dog is called a **puppy**.
Several **puppies** are often born
in a group, called a **litter**.

Puppy

A **puppy** is born with lots of
fur. It cannot see or hear.
It feeds on its mother's milk.

Two babies born together are called twins. Three babies born together are called triplets!

After two weeks, a **puppy** can see and hear.
It starts to walk about.

A **puppy** grows slowly.
It takes nearly a year to grow as big as its mother.

• How long does it take for a human baby to grow as tall as its mother?

A young bird grows inside
an egg. When it is big
enough, it hatches.

Chick

The young bird is
called a **chick**.
Some **chicks** have fluffy feathers.
Some have no feathers at all!

Nest

Many birds care for their **chicks** in a **nest**. They feed the **chicks** worms and insects.

After a few weeks, a **chick** grows new feathers that will help it to fly. Then the **chick** will leave the **nest**.

A duckling is a young duck. It can swim soon after it hatches.

• What must a chick grow or learn before it is an adult?

Young **frogs** start as eggs.

The adult **frogs** lay the eggs in a lumpy jelly called **frogspawn**.

Small, brown **tadpoles** hatch from the eggs.

Frogspawn

Tadpoles have tails like fish and live under the water.

16

The **tadpoles** grow front and back legs. They lose their tail.

Now they are **froglets**. They look like small adult **frogs**.

Adult **frogs** live on land and in water.

• Tadpoles use their tails to swim. How do adult frogs swim?

A **butterfly** changes all through its life.
It starts growing inside a tiny white egg.

A **caterpillar** hatches out of the egg.
It eats and eats.

A fat **caterpillar** looks very different from
its **butterfly** mother.

Caterpillar

The **caterpillar** builds a **pupa**.

Inside the **pupa**, the **caterpillar** grows into a **butterfly**.

Pupa

Now it has wings and a thin body.

Look how much it has changed!

Butterfly

• How many stages are there in a butterfly's life?

19

People are **humans**.
We are born.
We grow into adults.
We may have children.
Our children may have
their own children.

This is our **life cycle**.
A **cycle** means going
round and round.

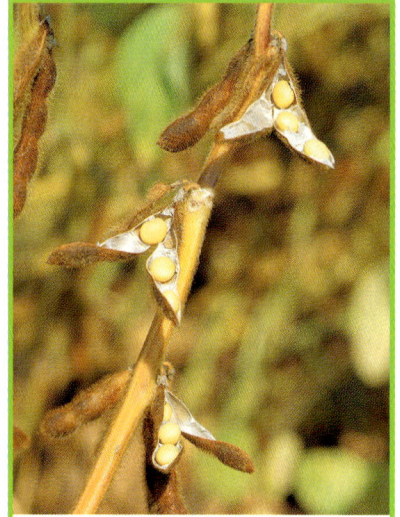

Plants have life
cycles, too. This
plant grows beans
that can grow
into adult plants.

Every animal has a **life cycle**. This **life cycle** never changes.

Joey

So an animal always grows in the same way.

You can only grow into a **human**.

A joey can only grow into a kangaroo.

• Can you think of any stages in the life of a plant?

Some animals grow
old like humans.

An elephant may **live** for over 70 years.
It keeps growing all its life.
Its tusks get longer and longer.

Most animals do not **live** as long as humans.

Many flies **live** for only a few weeks. A rabbit **lives** only for a few years.

Like humans, a male gorilla's hairs turn white as he grows older.

• How do people change as they grow old?

GROWING UP FAST

When Chloe and Clara arrived at Gran's house, Chloe couldn't wait to open her present.

It was a camera! Chloe smiled. "Happy **Birthday**!" said Gran. "Seven years **old** today. You've **grown** so big!"

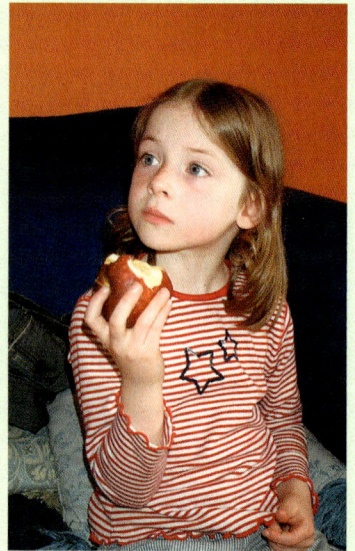

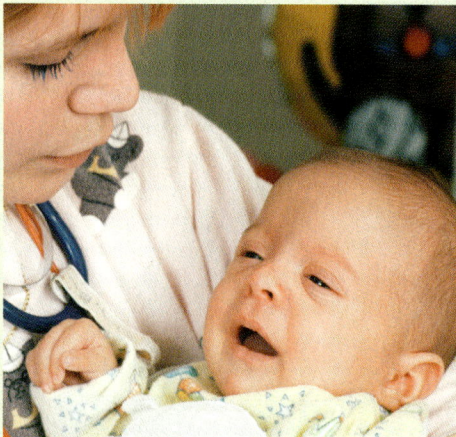

"When I was **born**, was I a tiny **baby**?" said Chloe. "Yes," said Gran. "You needed lots of **care**!"

24

"My dog Bella had a **litter** the same week," said Gran.

"Her **puppies** now have their own **puppies!**"

"So Bella is a Granny too," said Chloe.
"But she's only 11 years **old!**" said Clara.
"That's **old** for a dog," said Gran.

Later, they went into the garden to take pictures. A big **frog** jumped into the pond!

"Give it a kiss, Clara," said Chloe. "It might turn into a prince!"

"What's that jelly?" asked Chloe.
"It's **frogspawn**," said Gran.
"That's what we call **frogs' eggs**.
The **eggs** will **hatch** soon."

"I'll take pictures
as they **grow**
into **adults**,"
said Chloe.

"Look, that **mother
frog** is **laying** more
eggs," said Clara.

As Chloe bent over to take a picture, she slipped.

Clara grabbed
her just in time.

"Thanks," said Chloe.
"The pond is very slimy.
I don't feel like a swim!"

A few days later, the pond was full of wriggling shapes – **tadpoles!**

The girls watched them nibbling plants for food.

"Don't **tadpoles** need **milk** like **human babies?**" asked Chloe.

"No," said Gran. "Only **mammal babies** need **milk**."

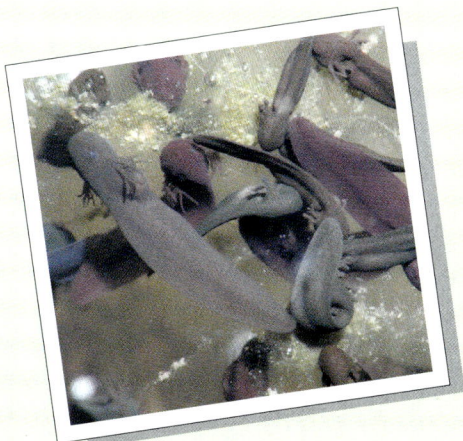

The weeks went by. The **tadpoles** ate and ate. They **grew** bigger and bigger.

Spring soon turned
to summer.
Caterpillars munched
on green leaves.
Butterflies fluttered
across the pond.

The **tadpoles** started to **grow** back legs.
Two weeks later, front legs appeared.
The **tadpoles** were turning into **froglets**.

One day, a big bird flew over the pond.
"It's a heron," said Gran.
"It likes to eat **frogs**."

"Let's stop it!" said Chloe.
"Lots of animals eat **frogs**," said Gran.
"That's why **frogs lay** so many **eggs**."

"The heron may have a **nest** nearby and needs to feed them to its **chicks**," said Clara.
"Yuck. I'm glad I'm not a **chick!**" said Chloe.

The **froglets** looked more and more like **frogs.**
"They'll be **adult frogs**
next year," said Gran.
"They will **lay** their
own **eggs.**"

"That's amazing,"
said Chloe.
"I'll have to wait a long time before I **grow** up."
"And a VERY long time before you **live** to
be as **old** as me!" laughed Gran.

Can you write a list of the stages in the life
of an animal such as a **frog** or **butterfly?**
Draw pictures to show its **life cycle.**

The caterpillar hatches
from an egg.

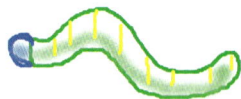

A butterfly crawls
out of the pupa.

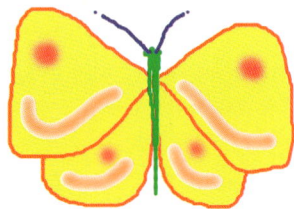

QUIZ

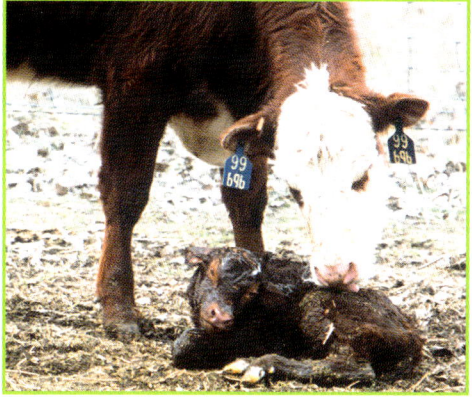

What group of
animals are **born**?

Answer on page 6-7

What different animals
hatch out of an **egg**?

Answer on page 8-9

Do these **young** have
parents that care for them?

Answer on page 11

Can you remember what these
young animals grow into?

Have you read this book? Well done! Do you remember these words? Look back and find out.

INDEX